20 FUN FACTS ABOUT THE GREAT PYRAMID

By Kristen Rajczak

Gareth Stevens
Publishing

Please visit our website, www.garethstevens.com. For a free color catalog of all our high-quality books, call toll free 1-800-542-2595 or fax 1-877-542-2596.

Library of Congress Cataloging-in-Publication Data

Rajczak, Kristen.
20 fun facts about the Great Pyramid / by Kristen Rajczak.
 p. cm. — (Fun fact file)
Includes index.
ISBN 978-1-4824-0470-8 (pbk.)
ISBN 978-1-4824-0471-5 (6-pack)
ISBN 978-1-4824-0467-8 (library binding)
1. Great Pyramid (Egypt) — Juvenile literature. 2. Egypt — Antiquities — Juvenile literature. 3. Pyramids — Juvenile literature. I. Rajczak, Kristen. II. Title.
DT63.R35 2014
932—dc23

First Edition

Published in 2014 by
Gareth Stevens Publishing
111 East 14th Street, Suite 349
New York, NY 10003

Copyright © 2014 Gareth Stevens Publishing

Designer: Sarah Liddell
Editor: Greg Roza

Photo credits: Cover, p. 1 Patryk Kosmider/Shutterstock.com; p. 5 Matej Kastelic/Shutterstock.com; p. 6 DEA/A. DAGLI ORTI/De Agostini Picture Library/Getty Images; p. 7 Doctor Jools/Shutterstock.com; p. 8 Svetlana Privezentseva/Shutterstock.com; p. 9 Dorothy Puray-Isidro/Shutterstock.com; p. 10 DEA/A. JEMOLO/De Agostini Picture LIbrary/Getty Images; p. 11 Andrea Colantoni/Flickr/Getty Images; p. 12 Dudley C. Tennant/The Bridgeman Art Library/Getty Images; p. 13 Ian McKinnell/Photographer's Choice/Getty Images; p. 14 (granite) OlegSam/Shutterstock.com; pp. 14 (workers pulling stone), 15, 19 Dorling Kindersley/Getty Images; p. 16 Ilona Ignatova/Shutterstock.com; p. 17 WhiteHaven/Shutterstock.com; p. 18 photo courtesy of Wikimedia Commons, Pyramid of Khufu - Entrance.jpg; p. 20 DEA/A. VERGANI/Contributor/De Agostini/Getty Images; p. 21 WILL & DENI MCINTYRE/Photo Researchers/Getty Images; p. 22 aodaodaodaod/Shutterstock.com; p. 23 Patrick CHAPUIS/Contributor/Gammo-Rapho/Getty Images; p. 24 Sylvain Grandadam/Photographer's Choice/Getty Images; p. 25 Andrew Zarivny/Shutterstock.com; p. 26 Mark Yarchoan/Shutterstock.com; p. 27 (Pyramid IV) Zai Aragon/Shutterstock.com; p. 27 (Pyramid of the Sun) Anna Omelchenko/Shutterstock.com; p. 27 (Pyramid of the Moon) ChameleonsEye/Shutterstock.com; p. 27 (Great Pyramid of Cholula) NCG/Shutterstock.com; p. 27 (Pyramid V) Gudmund/Shutterstock.com; p. 29 Dudarev Mikhail/Shutterstock.com.

Printed in the United States of America

CPSIA compliance information: Batch #CW14GS: For further information contact Gareth Stevens, New York, New York at 1-800-542-2595.

Contents

Words in the glossary appear in **bold** type the first time they are used in the text.

Into the Past

On the Giza **Plateau** near the Nile River, three huge pyramids rise towards the clouds. A short distance away is Cairo—one of the largest and busiest cities in Egypt. But out on the desert sands surrounding the Pyramids of Giza, the ancient world of **pharaohs** and their **dynasties** seems much closer than the bustling city.

The largest of the Pyramids of Giza is called the Great Pyramid. It's one of the seven wonders of the ancient world!

A pyramid is a structure with a square base and four triangular sides that slope up and meet at a point. The Pyramids of Giza are amazing examples of this kind of man-made structure!

FACT 1

The Pyramids were houses for dead pharaohs and were meant to last forever.

The Pyramids in Egypt were royal **tombs**. Similar to a healthy person buying a grave plot today, the pharaohs began to plan for their own death long before it happened! Their pyramid also served as a monument to their greatness.

burial chamber in the Step Pyramid of Djoser

The Great Pyramid had all the comforts of life in it, including food, furniture, and gold for the pharaoh's soul!

A pyramid's shape may have been meant to help the pharaoh reach the heavens.

Pharaohs were considered part god. After death, their body would be placed inside a pyramid. Passageways leading up and out, along with the sloping sides of the Pyramids, may have been made to help a pharaoh's spirit travel to be with the gods.

FACT 3

The first Egyptian pyramid looks like a huge set of stairs.

The pharaoh Djoser (ZHOH-suhr) had the Step Pyramid constructed around 2630 BC. A man called Imhotep likely **designed** it, making the inside look like Djoser's palace. It was about 200 feet (61 m) tall and one of the first all-stone buildings in Egypt.

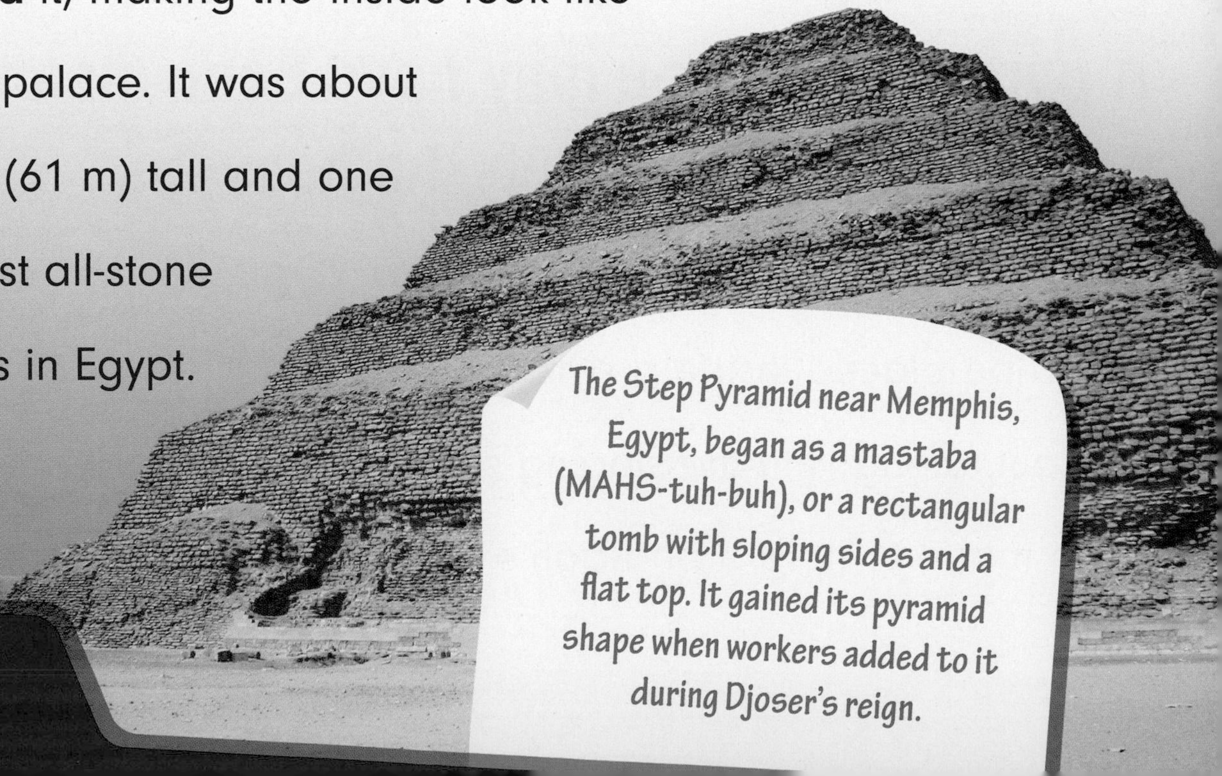

The Step Pyramid near Memphis, Egypt, began as a mastaba (MAHS-tuh-buh), or a rectangular tomb with sloping sides and a flat top. It gained its pyramid shape when workers added to it during Djoser's reign.

Notice the people at the base of the Great Pyramid. This gives you an idea of how huge it is.

FACT 4

The Great Pyramid was built more than 4,500 years ago.

Egyptians built pyramids for about 2,700 years. The three Pyramids of Giza were constructed over the course of about 110 years, between 2575 BC and 2465 BC. The Great Pyramid was built around 2550 BC.

The Great Pyramid is sometimes called the Pyramid of Khufu.

The second pharaoh in Egypt's Fourth Dynasty, Khufu (KOO-foo) ruled for about 23 years. He became pharaoh after his father, Snefru, died. He was married three or four times. Not much else is known about him, aside from the magnificent pyramid he left behind.

This ivory statue of Khufu was discovered in 1903. Experts think it was made many years after Khufu's death.

The three small step pyramids at the lower left were likely tombs for Menkaure's wives. They are called the queens' pyramids.

Pyramid of Khufu

Pyramid of Khafre

Pyramid of Menkaure

FACT 6

The other major pyramids of Giza were built by Khufu's son and grandson.

Khufu's son Khafre (KAHF-ray) built the middle Pyramid, known as the Pyramid of Khafre. The Pyramid of Menkaure (mehn-KOW-ray) is the southernmost of the three Pyramids. It's named for Khufu's grandson, the fifth pharaoh of the Fourth Dynasty.

FACT 7

Historians think up to 30,000 people helped build the Pyramids.

A Greek historian named Herodotus wrote that about 100,000 slaves built the Great Pyramid—but he has since been proven wrong. **Archaeologists** have discovered that only about 2,000 men worked at one time. And they were probably paid!

Many of the workers may have been farmers. During the time of year the Nile flooded their fields, they would work on the Pyramids.

Ancient builders left their mark on the Pyramids.

Discoveries of buildings near the Great Pyramid have shown that bakers, doctors, and priests lived among the workers. Some workers wrote **graffiti** on the Pyramids. From **hieroglyphics** inside the Pyramids, archaeologists learned workers were grouped into teams with names like "Friends of Khufu."

FACT 9

In total, the stone used to construct the Great Pyramid weighed about 5.75 million tons (5.2 million mt).

Roughly 2.3 million limestone blocks weighing about 2.5 tons (2.3 mt) each were brought from nearby **quarries** to construct the Great Pyramid. Some blocks may have weighed 16 tons (14.5 mt)! The pharaoh's burial chamber, however, is made of a stone called granite.

granite

Granite is harder and stronger than limestone.

We still don't know how workers moved stone from the quarry to the pyramid. Workers may have dragged stones on sleds—a cart with wheels would have sunk into the sand!

FACT 10

Archaeologists aren't sure how the Great Pyramid was built.

Most people accept that workers used ramps to move the blocks up to their place on the pyramid. What kind of ramp is still a mystery. Some think the ramp followed a snaking path around the pyramid, growing longer as the pyramid grew higher.

FACT 11

For more than 3,800 years, the Great Pyramid was the tallest structure on Earth.

The largest of the three Pyramids of Giza, the Great Pyramid was 481 feet (147 m) high when it was built. Today, it's dwarfed by many other structures, the tallest of which is the Burj Khalifa skyscraper in the United Arab Emirates.

Burj Khalifa

The Burj Khalifa is 2,722 feet (830 m) tall.

The limestone covering can still be seen on the peak of Khafre's pyramid.

FACT 12

Today, the Great Pyramid is about 30 feet (9.1 m) shorter than it was during Khufu's reign.

Khufu's pyramid used to be covered in smooth, white limestone. Some of the outermost layer weathered away. But much of it was stripped off to build the city of Cairo, revealing the pyramid's yellow core.

FACT 13

The pharaoh's sarcophagus, or stone coffin, was positioned almost exactly at the Great Pyramid's center.

In 2566 BC, Khufu's remains were placed in the main burial chamber at the pyramid's center. Then, the entrance to the pyramid was sealed! Two other rooms have been found. One has been called the "Queen's Chamber," though no queen was buried there.

This is the uncovered entrance to the Great Pyramid. Today, people most often use an entrance dug into the pyramid by robbers.

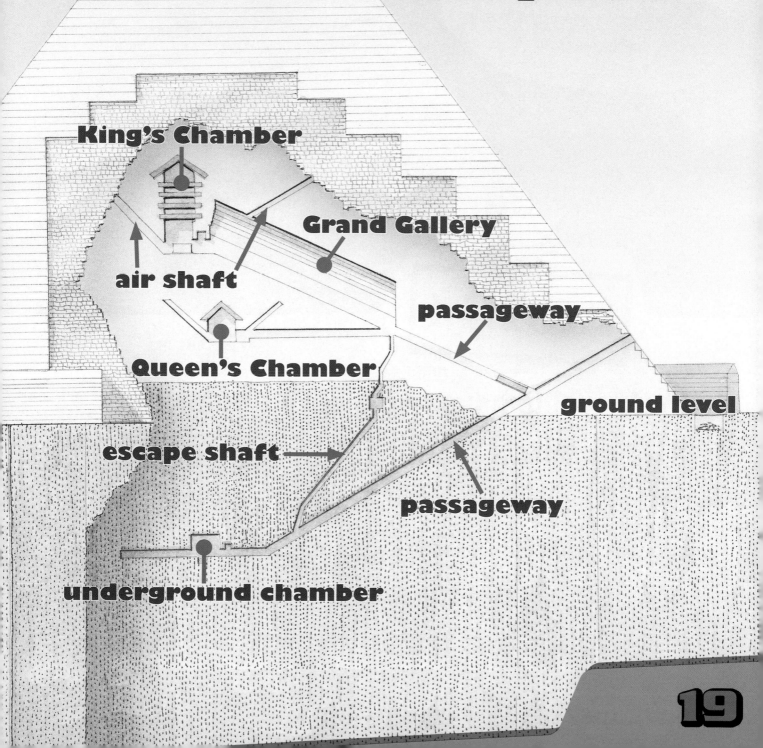

King's Chamber

Grand Gallery

air shaft

passageway

Queen's Chamber

ground level

escape shaft

passageway

underground chamber

Archaeologists know who many of the tombs near the Great Pyramid were for because of hieroglyphics on and inside them.

FACT 14

Khufu would have had plenty of company after death.

It took about 20 years to build the Great Pyramid. However, it doesn't stand alone! Small pyramids for members of Khufu's family and tombs for officials were built nearby. Raised roads connected the tombs to temples, and **canals** led to the Nile.

True or False?

Some people believe ancient Egyptian builders had help from extraterrestrials.

The Great Pyramid's four sides **accurately** face north, south, east, and west. But the compass wasn't invented yet! This fact and others have convinced many people that the Egyptians didn't have the knowledge to build so exactly. They think the Egyptians had help from **extraterrestrials**!

east

south

west

north

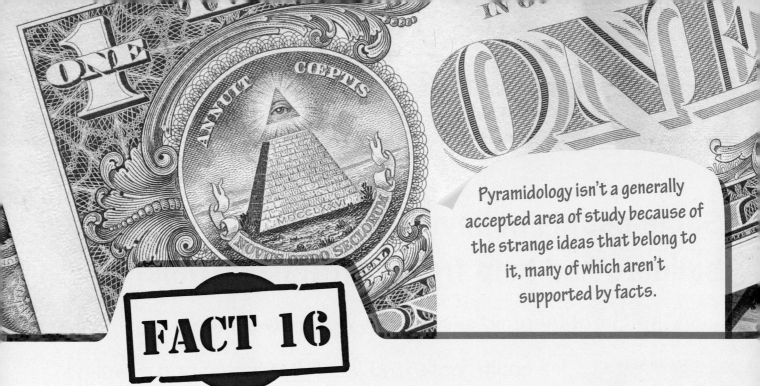

Pyramidology isn't a generally accepted area of study because of the strange ideas that belong to it, many of which aren't supported by facts.

FACT 16

Some pyramidologists believe the Great Pyramid predicted World War I.

Pyramidologists study pyramids, but most aren't interested in true scientific or historical discovery. For example, they've used the Great Pyramid's measurements to **predict** what year the world will end! Some believe the shape of a pyramid has special meaning, too.

FACT 17

Tomb robbers raided the Great Pyramid.

There used to be many more pyramids in Egypt, but most are simply piles of stone today. This is partly because of people stealing the bodies, gold, jewels, and other items placed inside these royal tombs. The Great Pyramid wasn't spared, though it still stands strong.

Khufu's burial chamber and sarcophagus, shown here, were empty when modern archaeologists found them.

23

FACT 18

In 2013, a group of Russian friends snuck to the top of the Great Pyramid!

Starting in the 1980s, Egyptian officials stopped people from climbing the Pyramids. However, in March 2013, a few people waited until night fell and climbed the Great Pyramid. They took pictures of the Sphinx and the surrounding desert from the top.

Some people still climb the Pyramids today even though signs tell them not to.

No Climbing

Can't visit Egypt? You can spend the night in the Luxor Hotel—a pyramid in Las Vegas, Nevada, that's 350 feet (107 m) tall!

FACT 19

Visitors often ride camels to get to the Great Pyramid.

While the Pyramids of Giza are near a big city, they aren't easy to get to! Also, only a few hundred visitors can tour the Great Pyramid every day—so if you want to see inside, you have to arrive early! You can hire a guide or explore on your own.

FACT 20

Central and South America have more pyramids than the rest of the world combined.

The Maya and other ancient people of the Americas used pyramids to house and **worship** their gods, though they sometimes buried kings inside, too. The pyramids were often centers of city life. The Maya built five pyramids in their great city of Tikal, found in modern-day Guatemala.

The pyramids in South and Central America were constructed differently, and on a smaller scale, than those in Egypt.

Pyramids of the Americas

The Great Pyramid of Cholula
Puebla, Mexico
177 feet (54 m) tall

Pyramid IV
Tikal, Guatemala
213 feet (65 m) tall

Pyramid of the Sun
Teotihuacán, Mexico
216 feet (66 m) tall

Pyramid of the Moon
Teotihuacán, Mexico
140 feet (43 m) tall

Pyramid V
Tikal, Guatemala
187 feet (57 m) tall

Timeless Treasures

Pyramid-like structures can be found in China, Greece, and India, among other places. However, none of these can compare in scale and grandness to the Great Pyramid. Similarly, today's man-made structures reach higher every year. They're impressive, but there's no mystery in their construction.

For thousands of years, the Great Pyramid has fascinated historians and scientists alike—and they make new discoveries about Egypt and pyramid construction all the time. There's no telling what we'll learn next!

The Pyramids of Giza were chosen as a World Heritage site in 1979. This means they will be protected for many years to come.

Glossary

accurately: with freedom from mistakes

archaeologist: a scientist who studies ancient buildings and objects to learn about past human life and activities

canal: a man-made waterway

design: to create the pattern or shape of something

dynasty: a series of rulers from the same family

extraterrestrial: a being not from Earth

graffiti: drawing or writing made on a public building without permission

hieroglyphic: part of a kind of writing that uses pictures

pharaoh: king

plateau: a raised area of land with a flat top

predict: to guess what will happen in the future based on facts or knowledge

quarry: an open pit commonly used for obtaining stone for building

tomb: a burial room

worship: to honor

For More Information

Books

Bramwell, Neil D. *Discover Ancient Egypt*. Berkeley Heights, NJ: Enslow Publishers, 2014.

Henzel, Cynthia Kennedy. *Pyramids of Egypt*. Edina, MN: ABDO Publishing, 2011.

Steele, Kathryn. *Stones and Bones: Archaeology in Action*. New York, NY: PowerKids Press, 2013.

Websites

Pyramids
www.pbs.org/wgbh/nova/pyramid/
Read more about the ancient Egyptians, and learn lots of great facts about the Pyramids on this interactive website.

Tombs of Ancient Egypt
video.nationalgeographic.com/video/kids/people-places-kids/egypt-tombs-kids/
Watch a video about the ancient Egyptians and their tombs.

Index